WHAT IS CANCER?

a guide to understanding cancer

Ashland Academy & Leia's Kids Foundation Present...

WHAT IS CANCER?

a guide to understanding cancer

ASHLAND ACADEMY

R E A D   W R I T E   L E A R N   G R O W

 a division of Bell Asteri Publishing

bellasteri.com

**BRINGING JOY TO
FAMILIES BATTLING
CHILDHOOD CANCER.**

leiaskids.org

This book belongs to:

_____

WHAT IS CANCER?

Cancer is a word that is used for more than 200 different diseases. These diseases are classified as a cancer because of their ability to spread from one organ to other organs.

IN THIS BOOK:

 You will learn about cells.

 You will learn about cancer cells.

 You will learn about cancer treatments.

 You will learn about cancer research.

 You will find out how you can help end cancer.

CELLS

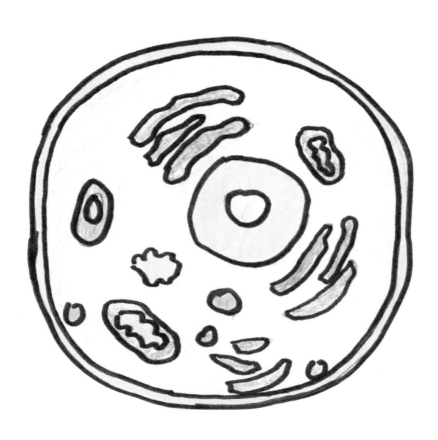

CELLS

Everything that is alive is made up of cells. Cells are so tiny that you cannot see them unless you use a microscope.

Plants are made up of cells.
Animals are made up of cells.
Humans are made up of cells.

Humans are made of more
than 75 trillion cells!

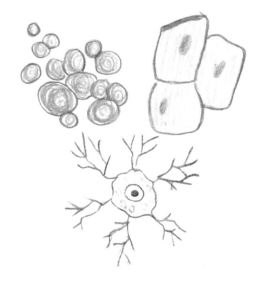

Cells come in many shapes
and have various functions.

People begin when two cells come together. Once those cells come together, they begin to divide and create new cells. Before long, a full human body has been formed!

Cell division happens super fast!

Pretty soon, those cells form all the parts of the human body.

Some cells become the brain

Some cells become the heart

Some cells become the kidneys

Some cells become the lungs

Some cells become the blood

Some cells become the bones

Some cells become the skin

What are some other organs in
the body that cells have formed?

 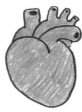 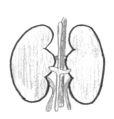 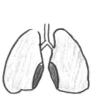 

CANCER CELLS

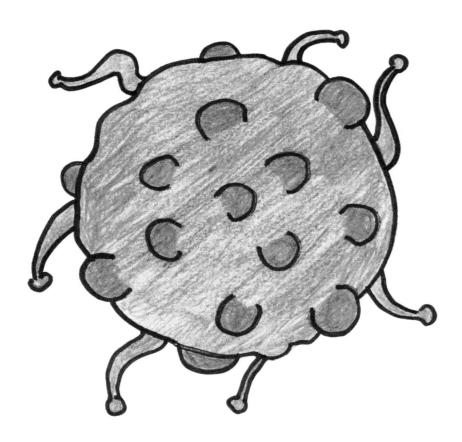

Most of the time, cell division goes pretty smoothly. But sometimes, the cells divide way too fast and they start getting all clumped together.

When this happens, the cells form a tumor.
A **tumor** is sometimes called a lump or a mass.

Tumors can be...

BENIGN or
MALIGNANT

See all the cells clumped together?
They made a tumor.

Benign

means that a tumor is not cancer. It cannot spread to anywhere else in the body. It might need to be removed with surgery or it might need another type of treatment, but it does not have the power to spread to any other part of your body.

Malignant

means that a tumor is cancer. It can spread to other parts of your body and make you very sick. If someone has a malignant tumor, they have to get help from a doctor to get rid of the tumor so it stops spreading and doesn't make the person even sicker or die.

There are several ways that doctors can determine if cells are benign or malignant. They include...

BIOPSY

SURGERY

CT SCAN

MRI

PET SCAN

BONE SCAN

X-RAY

*Do you know what the above words mean?

DIAGNOSING CANCER

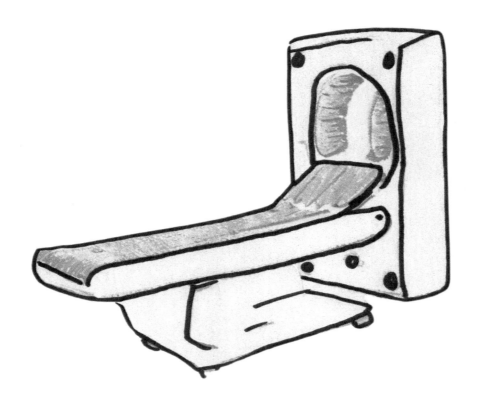

BIOPSY

A biopsy is when the doctor takes a sample of some tissue from the cells to look at them under a microscope. When they look through the microscope, they can see if the cells are bad (malignant) or no cancer is in them (benign). The biopsy is done by inserting a needle into a lump. Usually the patient is awake for this procedure. It is not painful, just a bit uncomfortable.

SURGERY

When doctors do a surgery, they make sure the patient is in a very deep sleep so they don't feel anything happening. Then, they make a small cut to get to the tumor and they remove it for a biopsy.

SCANS

There are many types of scans and they do not hurt the patient. The patient has to be very still when they are having a scan. Here are some types of scans cancer patients do:

- CT Scan - Some people say "cat scan" for this, but it has nothing to do with cats. It means "computed tomography" and it lets doctors have a really detailed look inside the body.
- MRI - This stands for "magnetic resonance imaging" and it is similar to a CT scan, but it gives an even more detailed look into what is happening inside the body.
- PET scan - This might make you think about pets, but it has nothing to do with the animals you love. PET stands for "positron emission tomography." To do this test, the doctor uses a special dye to show the changes inside the body. Using this scan, doctors get the most detailed look into the body to see where all the cancer cells might be.
- Bone scan - Just like the other scans, a bone scan takes pictures of the bones and can see deep inside the bones to look for cancer.
- X-Ray - X-rays are the simplest scans of the body and they can see inside so the doctor can look at the bones and internal organs. These photos do not give a super detailed look inside which is why doctors might start with an X-ray and then send the patient for the other scans to get a better, more detailed look inside.

WHERE CAN CANCER BE LOCATED IN A BODY?

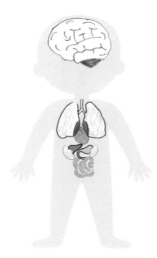

Cancer can begin in any organ in the body. Where the tumor first forms is the type of cancer a person has. If the tumor starts in the skin, it is a skin cancer. If the tumor starts in the blood, it is a blood cancer. If the tumor starts in the brain, it is a brain cancer. Any organ can develop cancer and wherever it first develops determines the type of cancer it is.

METASTASIZE

The word **metastasize** is a very big word that simply means "to spread". Cancer is made of very fast growing cells and can very quickly spread from one organ to another. When this happens, the cancer is more difficult to get rid of and more dangerous. If cancer starts in the skin and spreads to the brain, it is still a skin cancer, but it is a skin cancer that has metastasized (spread) to the brain.

Answer the following:

- If someone's cancer started in the lungs, what kind of cancer is it?
- If someone has lung cancer that metastasizes to the liver, what kind of cancer is it?

DOCTORS TREATMENTS & RESEARCH

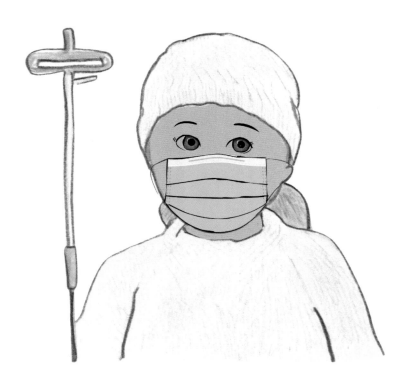

ONCOLOGIST

A doctor who treats patients with cancer is called an oncologist. This is a special type of physician who studies cancer and only works with cancer patients to make their cancer go away.

A pediatric oncologist is a doctor who treats children with cancer.

TREATMENTS

Because cancer can spread and become aggressive, the oncologist has to decide what kinds of treatments to do to make it go away. There are many options for treatments depending on what type of cancer it is and how much it has spread.

Have you heard of any of the following words?

SURGERY

CHEMOTHERAPY

RADIATION

BONE MARROW TRANSPLANT

IMMUNOTHERAPY

HORMONE THERAPY

CLINICAL TRIAL

SURGERY

Just like surgery to perform a biopsy, when a patient undergoes surgery to remove cancer, they are put to sleep and they do not feel anything happening. Sometimes doctors can remove a tumor through surgery and that gets rid of the cancer completely. Sometimes after surgery, the doctor will determine that only some of the cancer is out of the body and the patient might have to do more treatments.

CHEMOTHERAPY

Chemotherapy is medicine that destroys fast growing cells. Usually chemotherapy is given to a patient through an IV so that it goes quickly into the patient's bloodstream. It works through the body to kill all of the fast growing cells. And since cancer is fast growing, it works fast to kill the cancer cells.

A lot of patients lose their hair when they are on chemotherapy. The good news about hair is that it grows back!

RADIATION

Radiation therapy uses a machine to inject a radioactive substance into a tumor to try to kill the cancer. Patients go into a special room with the doctors and nurses and they carefully put them on a table. The patient must be very still and just lay on that table until radiation is finished.

BONE MARROW TRANSPLANT

A bone marrow transplant replaces cancer cells with non-cancerous cells that can grow healthy, new cells. Sometimes a patient will need a donor, someone who donates their bone marrow to them and other times, doctors can use the patient's own bone marrow for the procedure. Before the procedure, the patient has to do some chemotherapy and maybe some radiation therapy to prepare.

Bone marrow transplants are very complex. One of the greatest gifts someone can give is to donate their blood or their bone marrow. You can become a donor when you are an adult. But there are some children who can donate their bone marrow if they have a brother or sister who has to have a transplant. Doctors always do their best to make sure the donor and the patient feel as comfortable as possible.

For anyone 18 or older, scan the QR code and find out how you can help save a life. You just might BE THE MATCH for someone in need of a bone marrow transplant.

IMMUNOTHERAPY

Immunotherapy uses the body's own immune system to fight cancer cells. It is also used to help control side effects from other cancer treatments. Immunotherapy uses substances that are naturally in the body to boost the immune system. This way, the body is able to destroy cancer cells more effectively. There are almost no side effects with immunotherapy.

HORMONE THERAPY

Hormone therapy slows or stops the growth of cancer that uses hormones to grow. Hormone therapy is also called hormonal therapy, hormone treatment, or endocrine therapy

CLINICAL TRIAL

Clinical trials are ways to test new treatments and therapies to find, prevent, and treat cancer. They help researchers develop better treatments that are meant to improve the quality of life for people with cancer. They also test ways to help with the side effects of cancer and its treatment.

WHAT IS CANCER RESEARCH?

Cancer research is a way to look for and find better ways to prevent, diagnose, and treat cancer. Researchers are people who study cancer. Some researchers are also physicians who treat patients while others work in a lab to study tumor development and try to find therapies that will kill cancer cells.

Every day, researchers spend many hours studying cancer and trying to do a better job of preventing, diagnosing and treating it.

Prevention means that they are trying to figure out what causes cancer so that they can help people not even get cancer in the first place. Over the years, researchers have learned a lot about prevention. They learned that smoking causes cancer. They learned that using tanning beds causes cancer. They have learned a lot about many different environmental factors that cause cancer.

Diagnosing means that researchers are always looking for better ways to diagnose cancer – to find out if someone has cancer and if so, what kind they have. They have developed scans and screenings (tests that people do in a doctor's office to see if they have cancer). They are working hard to make it much easier to diagnose cancer so that it is easier to kill the cancer cells.

Treating cancer has come a long way over the years. In the beginning of the 20th century, almost everyone who got cancer died of cancer because there were no treatments that worked well. Today, there are so many wonderful new treatments that have been developed. You learned about many of these in this book. Today, researchers are working to develop even better treatments for cancer patients so that they can cure their cancer and live a great quality of life.

Did you know that cancer can happen to anyone? Cancer happens to old people and young people. It also can happen to pets. So, research is very important and thanks to researchers, people and animals are living much longer and healthier lives and we are seeing many more cures today. Much more needs to happen to cure all the cancer types. In the meantime, on the next page, there are some super cool words that cancer patients love to hear and YOU can help even more patients hear those words...

REMISSION

Remission is a word we use to mean that the cancer is no longer active. The patient might still have to do treatments because remission doesn't mean the cancer is gone. It just means the cancer is not spreading right now and is not actively doing anything.

NED

A lot of patients use the word "NED" and you might see them act very happy to say it. It stands for No Evidence of Disease and it means that the patient appears to have no cancer cells in their body at all.

CURE

The happiest word in the cancer community is the word "cure". Many types of cancer can be cured today thanks to lots of research and better treatments. There are still many other types of cancer that cannot be cured, but even those cancers can sometimes be in remission or even NED.

WHAT CAN YOU DO?

Host a fundraiser to help bring more money to researchers.

Put together gift baskets for cancer patients.

Study medicine and become a doctor or nurse or researcher.

When you grow up, vote for politicians who will increase funds to help end cancer.

THANKS TO PEOPLE LIKE YOU, SOMEDAY CANCER WILL END!

Made in the USA
Coppell, TX
01 June 2024

32983174R00017